YOU MUST REMEMBER THIS

1956

MILESTONES, MEMORIES,
TRIVIA AND FACTS, NEWS EVENTS,
PROMINENT PERSONALITIES &
SPORTS HIGHLIGHTS OF THE YEAR

TO : _____

FROM : _____

MESSAGE : _____

_____

selected and researched
by
mary a. pradt

WARNER ⓦ TREASURES™

PUBLISHED BY WARNER BOOKS

A TIME WARNER COMPANY

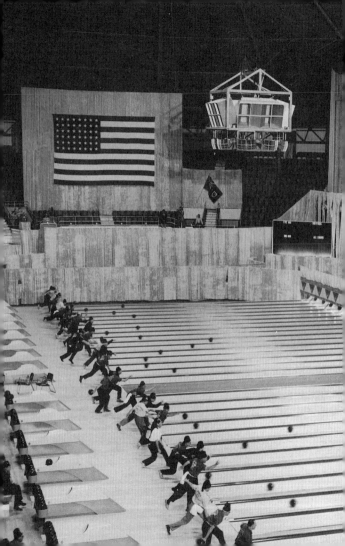

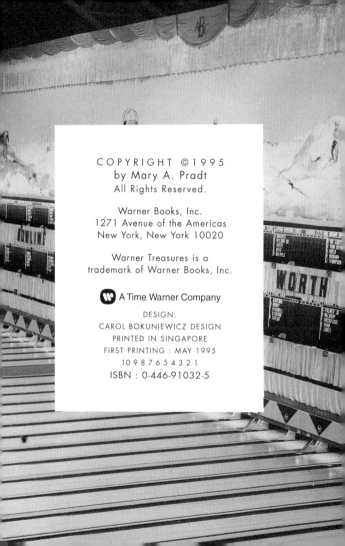

Warner Books, Inc.
1271 Avenue of the Americas
New York, New York 10020

Warner Treasures is a
trademark of Warner Books, Inc.

A Time Warner Company

DESIGN:
CAROL BOKUNIEWICZ DESIGN
PRINTED IN SINGAPORE
FIRST PRINTING : MAY 1995
10 9 8 7 6 5 4 3 2 1
ISBN : 0-446-91032-5

Civil rights and desegregation were major themes of
the year. In February, the Montgomery bus boycott,
inspired by **Rosa Parks**'s refusal to move to the back
of the bus, was launched. Ninety Black leaders were
arrested in Montgomery. Reverend Martin Luther King,
Jr., was found guilty of organizing the boycott. Also in
Alabama, there was conflict when the University of
Alabama, ordered to accept Black student Autherine
Lucy, instead expelled her. Bus segregation and the
Black boycott in Montgomery ended in December.

President Dwight Eisenhower underwent surgery in June for an intestinal blockage, but was able successfully to capture a second term, with Richard Nixon as running mate. The landslide victory of Ike, 66, marked the first time in the twentieth century a Republican won two consecutive terms. Ike and Nixon beat the Stevenson–Kefauver ticket in the biggest landslide since FDR's 1936 victory over Alf Landon.

FLASH!

newsreel

THE U.S. POPULATION REACHED 166.7 MILLION ON JANUARY 1.

The nuclear-powered aircraft carrier Saratoga was commissioned at the Brooklyn Navy Yard. Budgeted at $207 million, it would hold 100 aircraft.

A United Air Lines DC-7 and Trans World Super Constellation collided over the Grand Canyon June 30, killing the 128 people on board the two planes.

headlines

Britain gave up the Suez Canal after 72 years in June. President Gamal Abdel Nasser nationalized the Canal and announced plans to build the High Aswan Dam on the Nile after Britain, the U.S., and the World Bank pulled out of the project.

A brief war flared up in November. The Israeli army, under Moshe Dayan, made a lightning-quick conquest of the Sinai Peninsula. The Israeli government then refused to move out of areas it occupied, despite UN urging.

4

In the USSR in June, **Khrushchev** denounced his predecessor, Joseph Stalin. The West long had thought Stalin a monstrous dictator, but it was strange to hear the Soviet "party line" saying it. Khrushchev was starting a liberalization of some Soviet policies.

TWO LINERS, THE SWEDISH STOCKHOLM AND THE ITALIAN ANDREA DORIA, COLLIDED OFF NANTUCKET JULY 27, LEAVING 50 DEAD OR MISSING. FORTUNATELY, 1,652 WERE RESCUED.

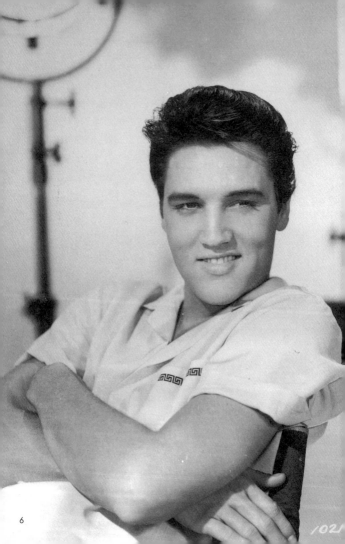

6

Elvis Presley, 21, performed "Heartbreak Hotel," "Don't Be Cruel," and "Blue Suede Shoes" for an audience of millions on "Ed Sullivan's Toast of the Town" September 9. He sang over a studio audience of screaming, weeping, shrieking teenaged girls. Some adult critics viewed Elvis's stage manner as "deeply disturbing." Said one fan, "He's just one big hunk of forbidden fruit."

HOT-RODDING WAS GROWING AS A NATIONAL PASTIME. DRAG RACING, ONCE CONSIDERED DANGEROUS ENTERTAINMENT FOR AMERICAN YOUTH, BECAME A SOPHISTICATED SPORT, WITH 350,000 HOT-RODDERS AND A MILLION SPECTATORS PARTICIPATING.

cultural
milestones

In May, there were crackdowns on the growing spring amusement of "**panty raids**," where rowdy collegians would appear en masse at dorms and sorority houses and collect underwear, usually from willingly participating coeds. The University of Kansas expelled 58 students in May for their raid on an Alpha Chi Omega sorority house at Baker University in Baldwin, Kansas. Also in May, at Berkeley, all male students were assessed fines of $3–$3.50, to help pay for the $10,000 damage done to sorority houses on that campus.

television

Don Herbert was enormously appealing, bringing science to a young audience, as "**Mr. Wizard**." In 1956, his audience was estimated at 5 million in 140 cities. There were more than 5,000 Mr. Wizard science clubs.

'56

This was the final season of "I Love Lucy."

Chet Huntley and David Brinkley began a 14-year association, anchoring the news on NBC.

9

Actress **Grace Kelly** wed **Prince Rainier II** on Apr 19 in the tiny principality of Monaco. Over 1,200 people including dignitaries from 25 nations, attended the Roman Catholic nuptials. The bride wore a gown of ivory taffeta which she donated to the Museum of Art in her home town of Philadelphia.

milestones

celeb weddings of the year

On June 29 in a civil ceremony, and on July 1 in a Jewish religious ceremony, playwright **Arthur Miller**, 40, wed actress **Marilyn Monroe**, 30. It was her third marriage, his second.

celeb births

KURT THOMAS, gymnast, was born March 29.

MARTINA NAVRATILOVA, tennis great, was born October 10.

WARREN MOON, quarterback, was born November 18.

JOE MONTANA, quarterback, was born June 11.

PHIL SIMMS, quarterback, was born November 3.

SUGAR RAY LEONARD, boxer, was born May 17.

MICHAEL SPINKS, boxer, was born July 29.

GERRY COONEY, boxer, was born August 24.

AMY ALCOTT, golfer, was born February 22.

BJORN BORG, tennis star, was born June 6.

LARRY BIRD, basketball legend, was born December 7.

DALE MURPHY, baseball player, was born March 12.

PROFESSOR ANITA HILL, accuser in Justice Clarence Thomas's confirmation hearings, was born July 30.

TOM HANKS, actor, was born July 9.

ROBBIE BENSON, actor, was born January 21.

ERIC ROBERTS, actor, was born April 18.

LISA HARTMAN, actress, was born June 1.

CARRIE FISHER, daughter of Eddie Fisher and Debbie Reynolds, was born October 21.

DELTA BURKE, comic actress, was born July 30.

DEBBIE BOONE, singer, was born September 22.

JAMES INGRAM, soulful singer, was born February 16.

PAUL YOUNG, singer, was born January 17.

PATTY SCIALFA, former E-Street Band member, now solo artist and wife of Bruce Springsteen, was born July 29.

Fred Allen, radio, TV, and film comedian, died March 17 at 61.

Louis Calhern, famed Broadway and Hollywood actor, died May 12.

Edwin Franko Goldman, popular conductor, successor to John Philip Sousa as best-known bandmaster, died February 21.

Irene Joliot-Curie, who won the Nobel Prize for chemistry along with her husband, and authored 54 books on scientific subjects, died March 17.

Alfred C. Kinsey, biologist/sexologist, founder of the Institute for Sex Research, died August 25.

Sir Alexander Korda, movie producer and director, died January 23. He's remembered for *The Private Life of Henry VIII*, *The Scarlet Pimpernel*, *The Third Man*, and *Richard III*.

Jackson Pollock, painter, known as "Jack the Dripper" for his unique painting style, died at 44 on August 11.

Babe Didrikson Zaharias, all-around athlete and Olympian, excelled in javelin, high jump, baseball, and several other sports, and won all the major women's golf events. In 1950 she was voted the premier woman athlete of the first half of the century. She died September 27.

56

1. **don't be cruel / hound dog** Elvis Presley
2. **singing the blues** Guy Mitchell
3. **the wayward wind** Gogi Grant
4. **heartbreak hotel** Elvis Presley
5. **rock and roll waltz** Kay Starr
6. **the poor people of paris** Les Baxter
7. **memories are made of this** Dean Martin
8. **love me tender** Elvis Presley
9. **my prayer** The Platters
10. **lisbon antigua** Nelson Riddle

hit music

Why Do Fools Fall in Love by the Teenagers, featuring Frankie Lymon, was a hit. Teresa Brewer, Gale Storm, and a duo called Patience and Prudence had 1956 hits.

11. **i almost lost my mind** Pat Boone
12. **the green door** Jim Lowe
13. **moonglow and theme from picnic** Morris Stoloff
14. **the great pretender** The Platters
15. **hot diggity** Perry Como
16. **i want you, i need you, i love you** Elvis Presley

Elvis. It was a great year for the "King of Rock and Roll." He made his first film, "Love Me Tender," in 1956, and he dominated the pop charts, with 18 charted singles during the year.

bestselling

fiction

1. **don't go near the water**
   by william brinkley

2. **the last hurrah**
   by edwin o'connor

3. **peyton place**
   by grace metalious

4. **auntie mame**
   by patrick dennis

5. **eloise**
   by kay thompson

6. **andersonville**
   by mackinlay kantor

7. **a certain smile**
   by francoise sagan

8. **the tribe that lost
   its head**
   by nicholas monsarrat

9. **the mandarins**
   by simone de beauvoir

10. **boon island**
    by kenneth roberts

books

1. **arthritis and common sense, revised edition**
   by dan dale alexander

2. **webster's new world dictionary of the american language, concise edition.**

3. **betty crocker's picture cook book, revised, enlarged 2nd edition**

4. **etiquette**
   by frances benton

5. **better homes and gardens barbeque book**

6. **the search for bridey murphy**
   by morey bernstein

7. **love or perish**
   by smiley blanton, m.d.

8. **better homes and gardens decorating book**

9. **how to live three hundred sixty-five days a year**
   by john a. schindler

10. **the nun's story**
    by kathryn hulme

The **Brooklyn Dodgers** and **New York Yankees** met, after their season-long struggle, in the World Series. Biggest thrill of the Series was Yankee right-handed pitcher Don Larsen, who achieved a no-hit, no-run perfect game in the sixth game of the battle with Brooklyn. The Yankees regained their championship much as the Dodgers had won it in 1955; both teams lost the first two games before coming back to win.

Coach Bud Wilkinson led Oklahoma to a 40-game winning streak. This beat a college football record dating from 1906 to 1914. Pro football had a successful season. The NY Giants, who moved from the Polo Grounds to Yankee Stadium, won their conference for the first time in a decade. The Giants went on to beat the Chicago Bears in the postseason playoff.

Horse Racing For the fourth year in a row, it was a $2 billion betting year. Two horses, Nashua and Swaps, got most of the attention.

Jackie Robinson decided to retire from baseball in December, after a trade to the New York Giants was announced.

sports

Cary Middlecoff won the U.S. Open for the second time, as Ben Hogan was beaten in his attempt at a record fifth Open win.

IN BOXING ROCKY MARCIANO RETIRED UNDEFEATED IN THE SPRING. FLOYD PATTERSON BECAME NEW WORLD HEAVYWEIGHT CHAMPION; AT 21, HE WAS YOUNGEST MAN TO WIN THAT TITLE.

Top Box-Office Stars of 1956

WILLIAM HOLDEN	MARTIN & LEWIS
JOHN WAYNE	GARY COOPER
JAMES STEWART	MARILYN MONROE
BURT LANCASTER	KIM NOVAK
GLENN FORD	FRANK SINATRA

Around the World in 80 Days, Mike Todd's multimillion-dollar widescreen spectacular, took best picture honors, as well as Oscars for best screenplay (adaptation), color cinematography, film editing, and musical scoring. **Yul Brynner** was named Best Actor for *The King and I.* **Ingrid Bergman** won as Best Actress for *Anastasia.* Best Supporting Actor was **Anthony Quinn** in *Lust for Life.* **Dorothy Malone** took Best Supporting Actress honors. Best scoring for a musical was *The King and I.* Best song was **"Whatever Will Be Will Be"** (*"Que Será, Será"*), from *The Man Who Knew Too Much.* Feature-length documentary honors went to ***The Silent World*** produced by Jacques Cousteau. Best Foreign Language Film (a new category) was *La Strada.*

Top Grossing Films of 1956 and their earnings

1. guys and dolls $ 9,000,000
2. the king and i $ 8,500,000
3. trapeze $ 7,500,000
4. high society $ 6,500,000
5. i'll cry tomorrow $ 6,500,000
6. picnic $ 6,300,000
7. war and peace $ 6,250,000
8. the eddy duchin story $ 5,300,000
9. moby dick $ 5,200,000
10. the searchers $ 4,800,000

Average weekly attendance at the movies was 47 million. This was up about 1 million over 1955.

THE AVERAGE COST OF ADMISSION WAS 49.7 CENTS.

movies

'56

cars

Cars were growing longer, sportier, and finnier. Lotsa chrome.

GM's new technical center was opened in May. In the sixtieth anniversary year of the auto industry, all the carmakers were expanding. The Big Three—GM, Chrysler, and Ford—had more than 96 percent of the first half's auto output. Willys and Kaiser dropped out of the passenger car business, to concentrate on utility vehicles, Willys becoming a subsidiary of Kaiser.

The station wagon

had become a preferred body style. In 1956, wagons cornered about 12 percent of the market, up from just 2.3% in 1947.

Ford introduced the Continental Mark II, a new prestige car in the $10,000 class. It was a two-door hardtop coupe with a hood extending back almost a third of its overall length of 18 feet.

The Cadillac car has always been a *great* favorite with the ladies. And for 1956, we feel certain that it will etch itself even more deeply in their affections. Certainly, they will take it to their hearts all the more for its great new beauty. Surely, they will have an even higher regard for the car insofar as interior luxury is concerned. And once they have driven it, we know they will have even greater admiration for Cadillac's magnificent performance. If you have counted Cadillac as *your* favorite, we suggest that you see and drive this latest version of the "car of cars" soon. We think you'll find that you've *admired* Cadillac long enough—and that the time has come to start *enjoying* one!

Cadillac

CADILLAC MOTOR CAR DIVISION • GENERAL MOTORS CORPORATION

Ceil Chapman

The year brought a "**romantic revival**," both in women's wear and in home decor. There was a trend away from stark simplicity. The Broadway success of *My Fair Lady* had an effect on fashion as well, recalling the Edwardian period. The beauty ideal was the peaches-and-cream complexion, with upswept hair, perhaps in a chignon.

fashion

The "**lady spy**" look, slinky and long-sleeved in black, was accessorized with a fabulous hat, perhaps plumed, maybe a jeweled turban. The bloused back and low-backed bodices gave "slouch" to the profile. Waistlines were kept high, for a long-legged look.

Fur was back in a big way. Mink collars accented suit jackets and evening costumes. Fox or lynx collars on day wear gave a luxe look. The sable-collared cloth coat or dinner suit was an important fashion statement. A mink wrap would work, too.

'56

final
factoid

NEW AND UNUSUAL WORDS CAME INTO USE IN 1956.
HERE ARE SOME OF THEM:

Barganza n.—a bargain sale

Brinkmanship n.—the international policy of
letting situations get to the brink of war before resolution.

Euratom n.—a projected European atomic pool.

Headshrinker n.—a psychiatrist—term dates to 1950,
but came into much wider use this year.

Roll on, roll off n. and adj.—a shipping process in
which large crates, railroad cars, and trucks are
rolled onto a ship at one port and off at another.

Sew-off n.—a final contest among home seamstresses.

Wolf-whistle v.t.—to whistle in a distinctive manner
denoting high approval.

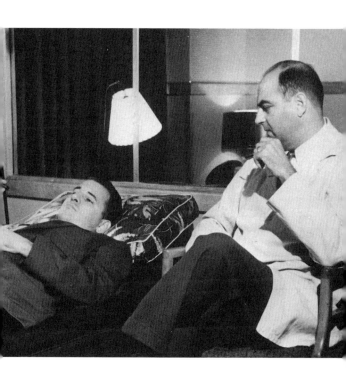

archive photos: pages 1, 4, 15, 25, inside back cover.

associated press: pages 2, 5, 10.

photofest : inside front cover, pages 6, 8, 9, 10, 13, 16, 18, 19.

original photography:
beth phillips: pages 13, 21, 22.

album cover:
courtesy of bob george/
the archive of contemporary music: page 13

photo research:
alice albert

coordination:
rustyn birch

design:
carol bokuniewicz design
paul ritter